THE ULTIMATE *SHARK* BOOK FOR KIDS

100+ Amazing Shark Facts, Photos, Quiz + More

Jenny Kellett

BELLANOVA

MELBOURNE · SOFIA · BERLIN

Copyright © 2023 by Jenny Kellett

The Ultimate Shark Book for Kids
www.bellanovabooks.com

All rights reserved. No part of this book may be reproduced in any form by any electronic or mechanical means including photocopying, recording, or information storage and retrieval without permission in writing from the author.

PAPERBACK
ISBN: 978-619-7695-88-5
Imprint: Bellanova Books

CONTENTS

Introduction **6**

Shark Facts **8**

Protecting our sharks **58**

Shark Quiz **64**

      Answers **68**

Word Search **70**

      Solution **72**

Sources **73**

THE ULTIMATE SHARK BOOK

INTRODUCTION

Sharks are one of the coolest and fiercest of the ocean's creatures. From the huge but gentle whale shark to the ferocious great white — sharks are the world's most fascinating fish.

Did you know that if you're afraid of sharks you are said to have galeophobia? But we're guessing if you're looking at this book, you don't have that, so let's get started!

SHARK FACTS

Sharks are some of the most exciting creatures on this planet! Let's take a look at some of the most amazing facts about sharks.

The deepest-diving shark is the Portuguese shark, which has been found over 9,000 feet (2743 m) below the surface of the ocean!

...

The first recorded shark attack was in 1749 in Havana, Cuba. British sailor Brook Watson, who later became mayor of London, was attacked while swimming. He survived but lost a leg.

A tiger shark.

Although the movie *Jaws* is not real, it was based on an actual shark attack in 1916, when four people were killed by a shark off the New Jersey coastline.

...

Almost 50 different species of shark have light-emitting organs called **photospheres**. They use this light for camouflage and to attract mates.

...

Sharks never run out of teeth; if they lose one, another one comes through from their rows and rows of backup teeth.

Sharks cannot eat puffer fish because the fish inflates like a balloon inside the shark's mouth.

...

Sharks sometimes eat other sharks!

...

Over its lifetime, a shark may grow and use over 20,000 teeth!

...

If you get bitten by a shark, they most likely won't bite you again. They don't like the taste of humans, so they let go once they realize you are not a sea animal.

A Caribbean reef shark.

Sharks can travel hundreds of miles in a day.

• • •

Although the average speed for a shark is around 20-40 mph (32-64 km/h), **mako sharks** can swim up to 60 mph (97 km/h)!

When a shark eats food that it can't digest (like a turtle shell), it can vomit by thrusting its stomach out its mouth and then pulling it back in!

• • •

Sharks aren't color-blind. In fact, some divers have claimed that they are attracted to specific colors, such as the yellow in some wet suits.

• • •

A shark's size is related to where it hunts for its food. Smaller sharks feed near the ocean floor, while larger sharks hunt in the middle ocean depths.

The **gestation period** (length of pregnancy) for female sharks can range from five months up to two years!

• • •

Sharks' skeletons are made from **cartilage**, not bone. This allows them to be more flexible. Cartilage is the same soft material that our ears are made of.

• • •

There's a type of shark called the **cookiecutter shark**. It gets its name from the fact that it can take ice-cream-scoop-shaped bites out of other sharks, including great whites!

Cookiecutter shark. *Image: NOAA Photo Library*

The skin of female sharks is much thicker than males. This is because males bite the females during mating.

• • •

Sharks' ears are located in their head.

• • •

Sound waves travel faster and further in water, so sharks can easily pick up lowpitched sounds made from movements such as by schools of fish.

<   *Blacktip reef shark.*

THE ULTIMATE SHARK BOOK

The **goblin shark** lives along underwater mountain ranges and outer continental shelves. They live in areas so deep that humans can't explore down there.

...

Sharks can heat up their eyes using a unique organ next to a muscle in their eye socket. This allows them to continue hunting in cold waters.

...

Shark fin soup is a delicacy in China.

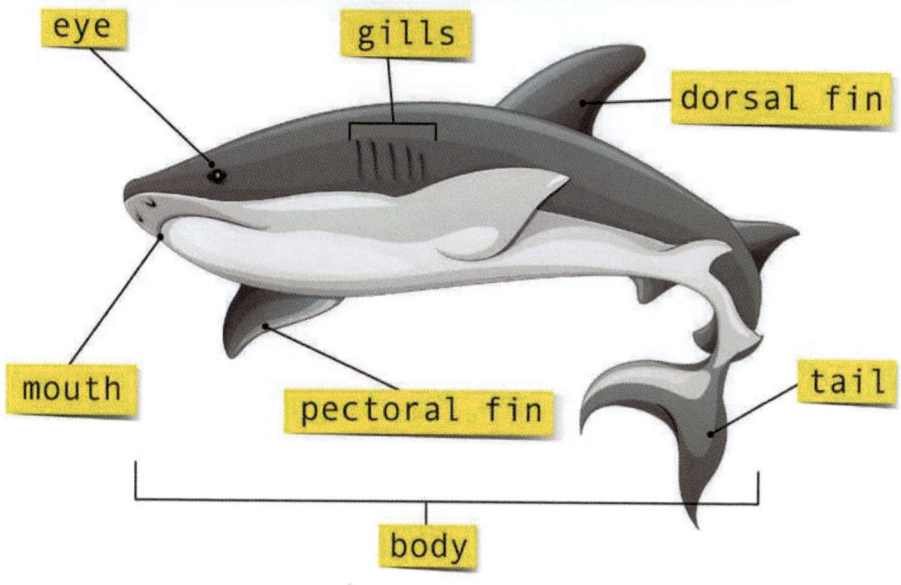

The prehistoric shark **megalodon** probably grew to 60 feet (18 meters). It is known today as the largest-ever shark.

• • •

Every year, great white sharks eat 11 tons of food! Humans eat around half a ton of food each year.

Almost two-thirds of shark attacks on humans have happened in less than six feet of water.

• • •

The **Greenland shark** is believed to be the slowest-moving shark in the world. It has been found with reindeer and polar bears in its stomach!

• • •

Sadly, humans kill around 73 million sharks annually. So they should be scared of us, not vice versa!

Greenland shark. *Image: Hemming*

Around 20% of sharks are close to extinction because of commercial fisheries accidentally catching sharks in their nets and on hooks.

Scalloped hammerhead.

Whale sharks lay the largest eggs of any animal on land or sea — the largest one ever found was 14 inches (36 cm) in diameter.

•••

Blue sharks are among the most endangered species in the world.

•••

Whale sharks are one of the largest species of sharks, but they do not pose a threat to humans as they only eat plankton.

•••

Hammerhead sharks are born with soft heads so that they don't damage their mother's birthing canal.

Divers swimming with whale sharks.

Although an almost equal amount of men and women swim in the ocean, around 90 per cent of shark attack victims are men.

• • •

Bull sharks have the most powerful bite force of all shark species. It is almost double that of the great white!

• • •

Only 20 species of shark are known to attack humans.

Bull shark.

Angel sharks, also known as sand devils, dig themselves into piles of sand and wait for unsuspecting fish to pass by before attacking them.

• • •

Sharks can hear a sound called *yummy hum*. This infrasonic sound is made by injured fish, so sharks know they can get an easy meal!

• • •

Sharks very rarely get cancer, which is why scientists study them looking for cancer cures.

Sharks have excellent hearing — some can hear their prey from up to 3,000 feet (914 m) away!

• • •

Whale sharks can live up to 150 years, which is longer than almost any other animal on the planet.

• • •

Sharks don't chew their prey. Instead, they tear it up into chunks and swallow it.

Sharks have remained almost the same for around 400 million years — that's since before dinosaurs were on Earth.

• • •

Baby sharks are called pups, male sharks are called bulls, and female sharks are just called females.

• • •

The small fins on both sides of a shark are called pelvic fins.

• • •

Most filter sharks, including basking sharks and megamouth sharks, dine only on plankton.

Close-up of a tiger shark.

THE ULTIMATE SHARK BOOK

The average tiger shark is 10-15 feet long.

• • •

Sharks have two chambers in their heart.

• • •

Some sharks must keep moving to keep water flowing over their gills; this process is called **ram ventilation**.

• • •

Some sharks have an extra set of eyelids called nictitating eyelids.

Fossilized shark's tooth.

Mako sharks can jump 20+ feet out of the water.

• • •

There are an estimated 10,000 great white sharks alive in the oceans today.

• • •

The great white shark cannot be eaten by humans because it contains high amounts of mercury.

Great white shark.

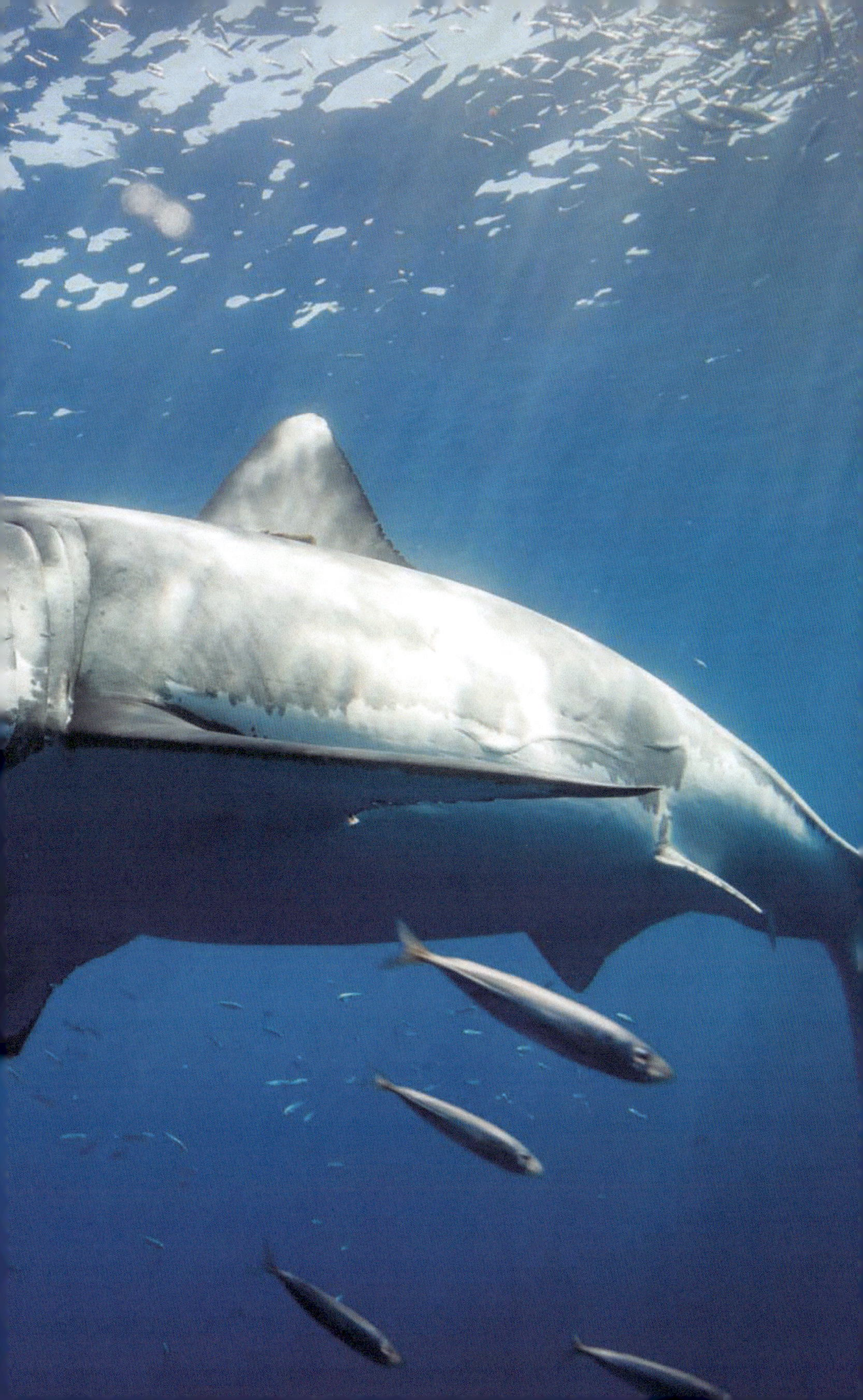

Sharks get oxygen to 'breathe' by filtering it from the ocean.

• • •

Oceanic whitetip sharks have rounded dorsal fins.

• • •

Less than 100 megamouth sharks have ever been seen by humans since their discovery in 1976 since they live so deep underwater. Their closest relatives are the whale shark and the basking shark, which are all filterfeeders.

Whitetip shark.

Frilled sharks have circular-shaped mouths.

• • •

Some shark pups eat their siblings before birth; this is called **intrauterine cannibalism**.

When attacking their prey, great white sharks' eyes roll into the back of their heads to prevent their eyes from being damaged.

• • •

Pygmy sharks can dive to depths of one mile and generate their own light.

• • •

Whale sharks have the largest mouths of all sharks.

• • •

Great white sharks typically grow to lengths of 12-16 feet (3.7-4.9 m).

A Great White shark eating a whale carcass.

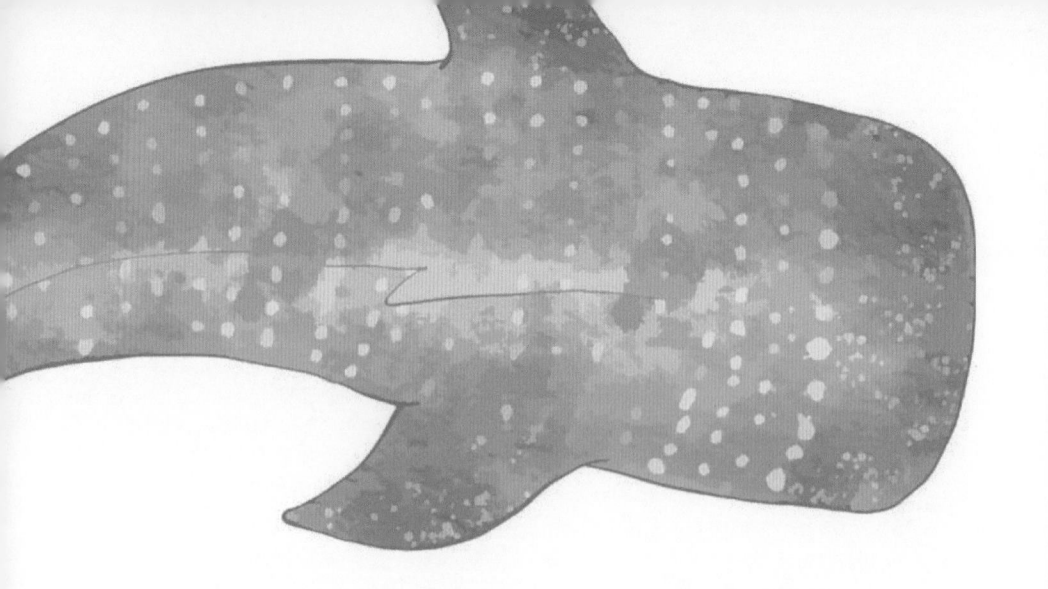

Great white sharks can survive for 3 months off of one big meal.

• • •

Some sharks can be put into a trance by flipping them upside down; this is called tonic immobility.

• • •

The United States has the most recorded shark attacks in history, with 1,563. Australia comes in second with 682 attacks.

A lemon shark. It gets its name from it's yellowish coloring, which works as a camouflage against the sand.

Although most sharks give birth to live young, a small number are oviparous, meaning they lay eggs.

THE ULTIMATE SHARK BOOK

Sand tiger shark.

Another name for the **sand tiger shark** is the grey nurse shark.

• • •

Female sharks are usually bigger than male sharks.

• • •

Blue sharks are known for eating so much that they vomit and then continue eating.

• • •

Thresher sharks use their long tails to stun their prey.

THE ULTIMATE SHARK BOOK

An epaulette shark. They are found in the warm, shallow waters off Australia and New Guinea. They can survive for hours without oxygen and even clamber across land to reach new areas of water.

There are over 500 different species of sharks.

• • •

Dwarf sharks are the smallest species of shark.

• • •

Great white sharks can leap 10 feet out of the water.

• • •

Only one drop of blood would need to be in an Olympic-sized pool before a great white could detect it.

Ichthyologist is the name for people who study sharks.

• • •

Bull sharks can survive in both saltwater and freshwater.

• • •

Sand tiger sharks gulp air to improve their hunting.

• • •

Silky sharks have smoother skin than other sharks.

Two silky sharks.

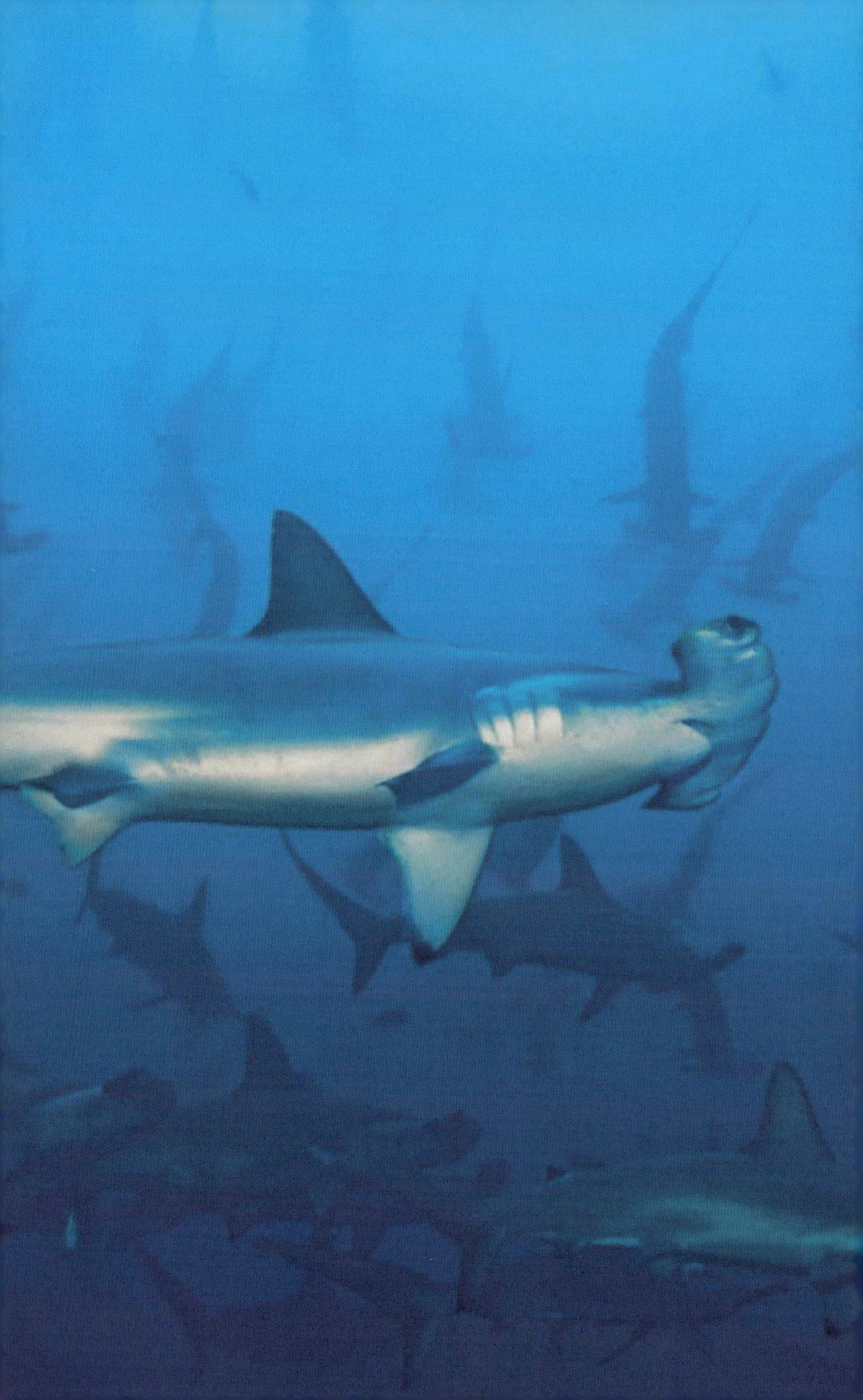

Sharks have around 3,000 teeth in their mouth at any one time.

• • •

Nurse sharks can sit still without drowning.

• • •

Manta rays also belong to the shark family.

• • •

Swell sharks evade predators by swallowing sea water until it doubles in size.

< *A school of hammerhead sharks.*

Leopard shark.

Great white pups can be up to five feet long.

• • •

Magnets, soap and the smell of dead sharks can all repel sharks.

• • •

The tail of a shark is called the **caudal fin**. Blue sharks are also known as Wolves of the Sea because of the way they like to hunt in groups or schools.

Great white sharks usually bite humans because they mistake them for seals.

• • •

The head of a hammerhead shark is called the **cephalofoil**.

• • •

Tiger sharks have a layer of tissue on their eyes called *tapetum lucidum* to help them see in low-light conditions.

Bull sharks are the most aggressive type of shark.

• • •

Nurse sharks are known to live longer than most other sharks in an aquarium.

• • •

If a great white shark and an orca whale were in a fight, the orca would win.

• • •

The swell shark, found in New Zealand, barks like a dog!

Nurse shark. *Image: Steve Laycock*

Sharks can be found in all of Earth's oceans.

• • •

Sometimes sharks attack metal objects in the ocean. This is because metal can give off electromagnetic signals, confusing sharks.

• • •

Great white sharks live along the coast of all continents except Antarctica.

• • •

Epaulette sharks can use their pectoral fins to 'run' along the ocean floor.

The great white shark gets its name from the color of its underside.

• • •

A fear of sharks is called **galeophobia**.

• • •

Most scientists believe that the purpose of the hammerhead shark's oddly-shaped head is to detect prey.

• • •

Amanzimtoti Beach in South Africa is the most dangerous beach in the world for shark attacks.

PROTECTING OUR SHARKS

Sharks are beautiful creatures and an essential part of the world's ecosystem, yet they are becoming increasingly endangered.

As shark lovers, it is our job to promote the protection of sharks.

Here are just a few reasons why we need to protect our sharks:

Sharks are being fished at a rate that's faster than they can reproduce.

• • •

Killing sharks can affect whole ecosystems, which rely on sharks to survive.

• • •

Sharks are a good indicator of how healthy an ecosystem is. If sharks start leaving an area, it is likely there will be problems with the other animals and plant life.

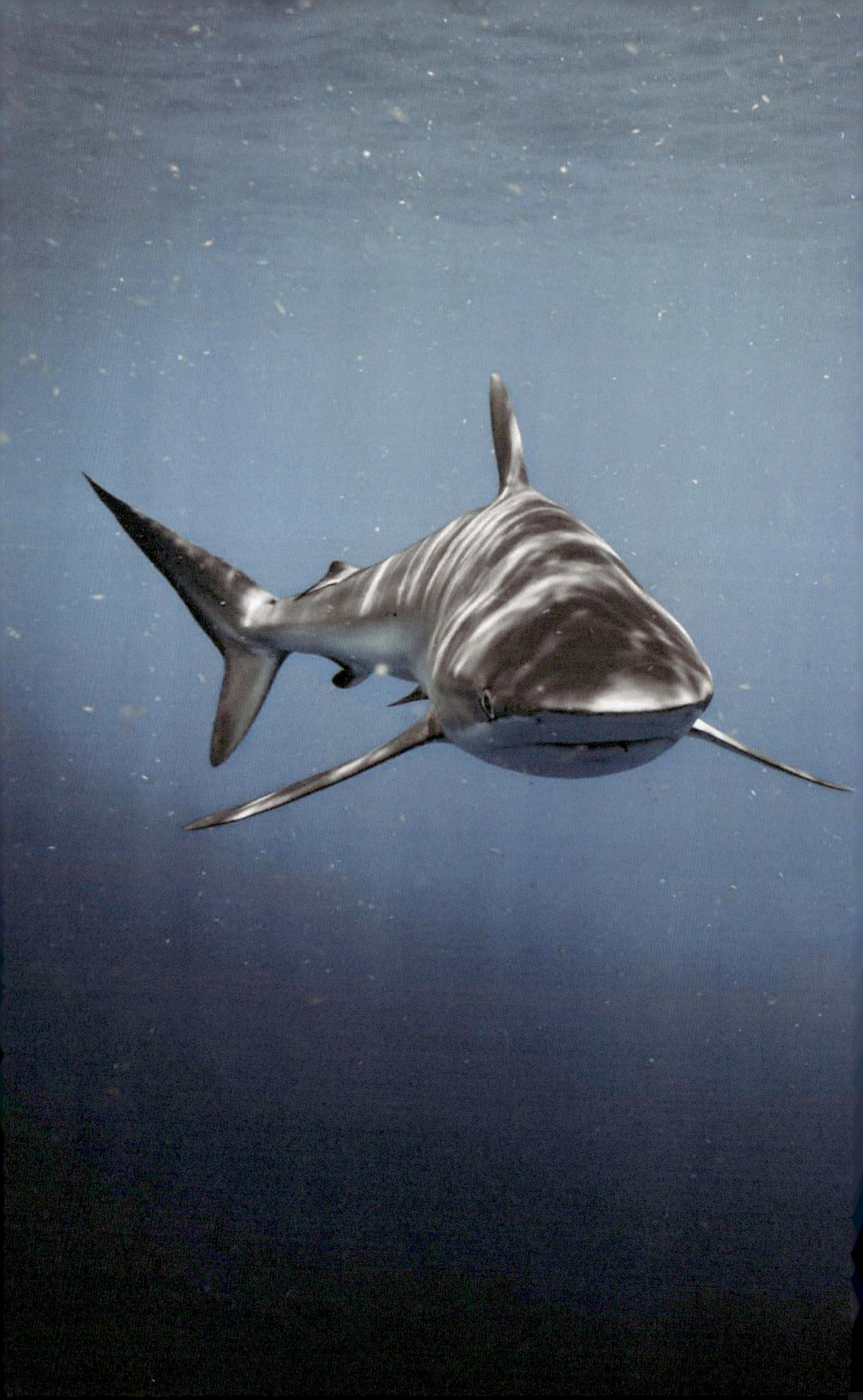

Many sharks prey on sick and weak fish. By doing this, they are often preventing diseases from spreading and keeping populations of those fish healthier.

...

Sharks have been around for over 450 million years. They are as entitled to live happily on Earth as we are!

HOW CAN YOU HELP SHARKS?

Sharks need help from people just like you to raise awareness of their problems.

You can support many organisations, including *Project Aware Foundation*, *Oceana Headquarters*, *Shark Angels*, *Shark Savers*, *the WWF* and *Predators in Peril*.

Through these organisations, you have opportunities to adopt a shark, donate money and learn more about other ways you can help.

A little goes a long way. Here are a few ideas:

- Instead of gifts on your birthday, ask your friends and family for donations to your favourite shark charity.
- Hold a bake sale to raise money.
- Be a shark ambassador! Share information about the problems sharks face on your social media and speak to friends and family to spread the word.
- Adopt a shark (virtually, of course!) through the organisations mentioned earlier.
- Check with your local zoo to see what projects they're involved in and how you can help.
- Celebrate **Shark Awareness Day** on July 14.

SHARK-QUIZ

Now test your knowledge in our shark quiz! Answers are on page 68.

1 In which country was the first recorded shark attack?

2 Which shark can swim up to 60 mph (97 km/h)?

3 Sharks are color-blind. True or false?

4 What are sharks' skeletons made of?

5 What was the largest-ever species of shark?

6 Which species of shark is the slowest moving?

7 Which sharks lay the largest eggs?

8 Which shark has the strongest bite force?

9 There are over 500 species of shark. True or false?

10 What are baby sharks called?

11 What do filter sharks eat?

12 Why can't humans eat great white sharks?

13 Which shark has the largest mouth?

Whale shark.

14   Which country has had the most recorded shark attacks?

15   How many chambers do sharks have in their hearts?

16   Are male or female sharks usually bigger?

17   What is the smallest species of shark?

18   What is someone who studies sharks called?

19   Which shark has the smoothest skin?

20   Manta rays are part of the shark family. True or false?

ANSWERS

1. Cuba.
2. Mako shark.
3. False.
4. Cartilage.
5. Megalodon.
6. Greenland shark.
7. Whale sharks.
8. Bull shark.
9. True.
10. Pups.
11. Plankton.
12. They contain too much mercury, which is poisonous.
13. Whale shark.
14. USA.
15. Two.
16. Female.
17. Dwarf sharks.
18. Ichthyologist.
19. Silky shark.
20. True.

Blacktip reef shark.

SHARKS
WORD SEARCH

```
Q W G R E A T W H I T E
Y B D B G D S I Y T R D
T A R O Z S D F G V C U
R S H A R K T R E E U Y
E K Q W D S B H G F R T
D I T R E W A S C X Z E
F N R M E G A L O D O N
G G E E B H G F D N H N
J H S R B U L L S D A B
H F D M J H F S D F Z R
O C E A N Z X C F D S E
B P T D E W A G J T D F
```

Can you find all the words below in the wordsearch puzzle on the left?

SHARK	TIGER	SONAR
DORSAL	MEGALODON	BULL
OCEAN	BASKING	GREAT WHITE

THE ULTIMATE SHARK BOOK

SOLUTION

	G	R	E	A	T		W	H	I	T	E
	B	D					I				
	A		O				G				
	S	H	A	R	K			E			
	K				S				R		
	I				A	S					
	N		M	E	G	A	L	O	D	O	N
	G							N			
				B	U	L	L		A		
									R		
O	C	E	A	N							

SOURCES

Shark - Wikipedia (2022). Available at: https://en.wikipedia.org/wiki/Shark (Accessed: 5 November 2022).

12 Shark Facts That May Surprise You (2022). Available at: https://www.fisheries.noaa.gov/feature-story/12-shark-facts-may-surprise-you (Accessed: 5 November 2022).

Learn our top 10 facts about sharks (2022). Available at: https://www.wwf.org.uk/learn/fascinating-facts/sharks (Accessed: 5 November 2022).

Signorelli, L. and Signorelli→, V. (2020) **Ten interesting facts about sharks - Australian National Maritime Museum, Australian National Maritime Museum**. Available at: https://www.sea.museum/2020/01/16/ten-interesting-facts-about-sharks (Accessed: 5 November 2022).

shark | Attacks, Types, & Facts (2022). Available at: https://www.britannica.com/animal/shark (Accessed: 5 November 2022).

The physical appearance of sharks (2022). Available at: https://www.britannica.com/summary/shark (Accessed: 5 November 2022).

shark (2022). Available at: https://kids.britannica.com/students/article/shark/277020 (Accessed: 5 November 2022).

AND THAT'S ALL, FOLKS!

We'd love it if you left us a **review**—they always make us smile, but more importantly they help other readers make better buying decisions.

Thank you again for your support!

Visit us at

www.bellanovabooks.com

for more fun fact books
and regular giveaways!

Also by Jenny Kellett

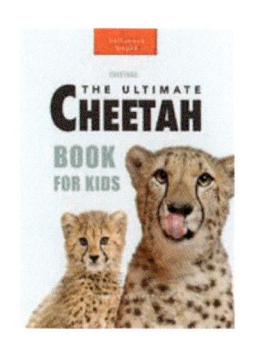

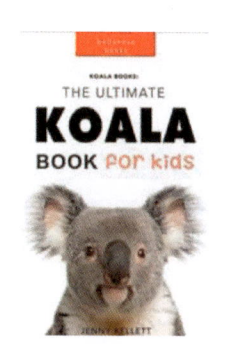

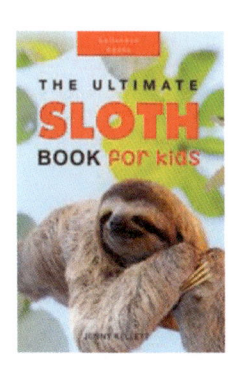

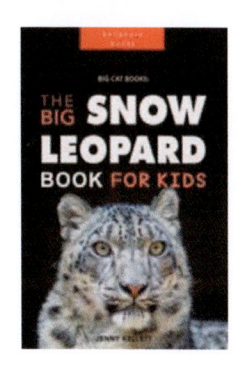

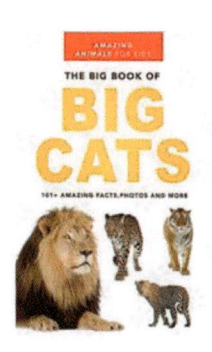

... and more!

Available at
www.bellanovabooks.com